This book

CORONA VIRUS DISEASE (COVID-19)

Awareness, Prevention and Management

is

Dedicated to my parent

Family members, mentors, friends, readers and well-wishers.

Specially dedicated to all frontline workers..

CORONA VIRUS DISEASE (COVID-19): AWARENESS, PREVENTION AND MANAGEMENT

A STEP TOWARDS AWARENESS AGAINST COVID-19

RITESH MISHRA

ISBN 979-888503756-3

Contents

Preface

This book ***"CORONA VIRUS DISEASE (COVID-19): Awareness, Prevention and Management*** " is designed to understand about Corona Virus and its impact on the human health so that together a step to fight against COVID-19 can be jointly carried out through awareness, prevention and management in systematic chain. This book is prepared to create awareness about the COVID-19, describe about available vaccines for vaccination and some other steps that can be helpful in tackling with this pandemic.

This bookis beneficial to the medical professional as well as students, common citizen and general people.

Acknowledgements

"A small support could accomplish a big dream."

I owe my sincere thanks to all hands that joined me during this journey and turn this dream into reality. I must be thankful to my parent, family, relatives, friends, teachers and all my readers and well wishers for being my strength. I would like to thank owner of related links, web page, government sites, journal & research paper presented with authentic information on the topic that really helped me in bringing this book namely ***"CORONA VIRUS DISEASE (COVID-19): Awareness, Prevention and Management "*** creatively. Bringing this book in your hand couldn't have been possible without support from my team of Global Star Healthcare World and Star Bharat Healthcare for standing besides us in all tough time. Last but not the least, Thank you everyone for your support, encouragement and guidance.

Though Sincere efforts have been made to verify the correctness of the text, however, in spite of best efforts, some mistakes related to human errors, some inaccuracies, ambiguities and typographic mistakes may have corrupt in. Therefore, I request all the readers to send their feedback and suggestions for improving the future editions of the book. Feedbacks received shall be highly appreciated and heartly acknowledged.

Kindly email at: riteshmishra4k@gmail.com

- Ritesh Mishra (Author)

ONE
CORONA VIRUS

Corona Virus

Corona viruses are a large group of viruses. **Corona virusesare** a family of viruses known for containing strains that cause potentially deadly diseases in mammals and birds.

CORONA VIRUSES

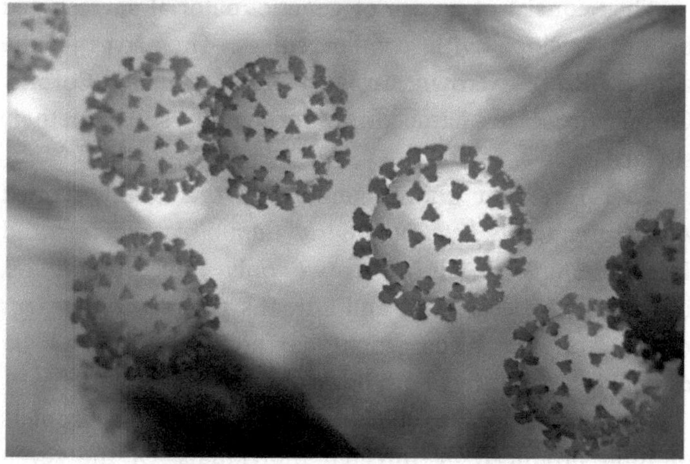

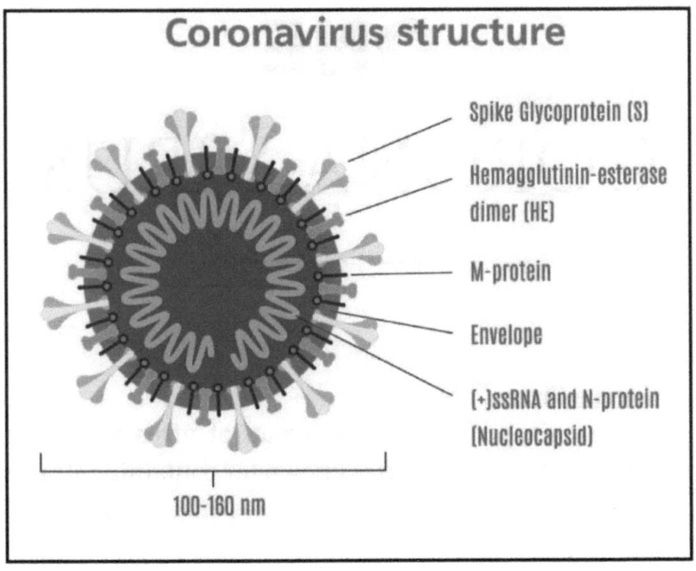

They consist of a core of genetic material surrounded by an envelope with protein spikes. This gives it the appearance of a crown. Crown in Latin is called Corona. Corona viruses are named for the crown-like spikes on their surface.

There are four known genuses in the family, named *Alpha coronavirus*, *Beta coronavirus*, *Gamma coronavirus*, and *Delta coronavirus*. The first two only infect mammals, including bats, pigs, cats, and humans. *Gamma coronavirus* mostly infects birds such as poultry, while *Delta coronavirus* can infect both birds and mammals.

In humans they're typically spread via aiborne droplets of fluid produced by infected individuals. Of the seven coronaviruses known to infect humans, four spread with seasonal regularity, causing anything from mild cold-like symptoms to flu-like discomforts. A few more notable strains, including SARS-CoV-2 (responsible for COVID-19, and those responsible for severe acute respiratory syndrome (SARS) and Middle East respiratory syndrome (MERS), can cause death in humans. The cause of death is complex, though is typically the result of heightened immune responses causing damage in multiple systems throughout the body.

Human corona viruses were first identified in the mid-1960s. The seven coronaviruses that can infect people. Common human coronaviruses are 229E (alpha coronavirus), NL63 (alpha coronavirus), OC43 (beta coronavirus) and HKU1 (beta coronavirus). Other human coronaviruses are MERS-CoV (the beta coronavirus that causes Middle East Respiratory Syndrome, or MERS), SARS-CoV (the beta coronavirus that causes severe acute respiratory syndrome, or SARS) and SARS-CoV-2 (the novel corona virus that causes corona virus disease 2019 or COVID-19).

People around the world commonly get infected with human corona viruses 229E, NL63, OC43, and HKU1.Sometimes corona viruses that infect animals can evolve and make people sick and become a new human coronavirus. Three recent examples of this are 2019-nCoV, SARS-CoV, and MERS-CoV.

Some symptoms of common human corona viruses are: runny nose, sore throat, headache Fever, cough as well as general feeling of being unwell. Human coronaviruses can sometimes cause lower-respiratory tract illnesses, such as pneumonia or bronchitis. This is more common in people with cardiopulmonary disease, people with weakened immune systems, infants, and older adults.

Common human corona viruses usually spread from an infected person to others either through the air by coughing and sneezing; close personal contact, like touching or shaking hands or touching an object or surface with the virus on it, then touching mouth, nose, or eyes before washing hands.

Sometimes, respiratory secretions are tested to figure out which specific germ is causing symptoms. **Testing for common human coronaviruses are mostly done through swab collected from mouth and nose.**In case, one is found to be infected with a common coronavirus (229E, NL63, OC43, and HKU1), that does not mean that s/he is infected with the 2019 novel coronavirus. There are different tests to determine if person is infected with 2019 novel coronavirus. The healthcare provider can determine if person should be tested or not.

Symptomatic treatmentis carried out for common human coronaviruses as there is no specific medicine available. However vaccine to protect against human coronaviruses are available nowadays for prevention of illnesses caused by human coronaviruses. Most people with common human coronavirus illness will recover on their own. However, to relieve symptoms:

- take pain and fever medications (Caution: do not give aspirin to children)
- use a room humidifier or take a hot shower to help ease a sore throat and cough
- drink plenty of liquids
- stay home and rest

Note: If you are concerned about your symptoms, contact your healthcare provider.

Preventing viral respiratory infections

1. Protect yourself from getting sick

- wash your hands often with soap and water for at least 20 seconds
- avoid touching your eyes, nose, or mouth with unwashed hands
- avoid close contact with people who are sick

2. Protect others when you are sick

- stay home while you are sick
- avoid close contact with others
- cover your mouth and nose when coughing or sneezing
- clean and disinfect objects and surfaces

Table showing History of Corona virus : Disease caused and causative agent

Disease	Cause	First identified	Details
Avian infectious bronchitis	*Avian coronavirus* (IBV)	1920s (isolated in 1938)	Originated from North America.
Transmissible gastroenteritis	Transmissible gastroenteritis virus (TGEV)	1965 (recognized in 1946)	Infects pigs, cats and dogs.
Common cold, pneumonia, bronchiolitis, etc.	*Human coronavirus 229E (HCoV-229E)*	1930s (isolated in 1965)	Likely originated from bats.
Murine encephalitis	JHM (named after John Howard Mueller), a murine coronavirus	1949	
Common cold	*Human coronavirus OC43 (HCoV-OC43)*	1967	Likely originated from rodents, then transmitted to humans through cattle.
Acute infectious diarrhea	*Porcine epidemic diarrhea virus* (PEDV)	1971	Caused outbreaks in 1972 and 1978, 2010, 2013, 2014, and 2015. Infects pigs.
Severe acute respiratory syndrome (SARS)	Severe acute respiratory syndrome coronavirus (SARS-CoV or SARS-CoV-1), a strain of *severe acute respiratory syndrome–related coronavirus* (SARSr-CoV)	2002	Caused the 2002–2004 SARS outbreak. Likely originated from horseshoe bats.
Common cold	*Human coronavirus HKU1 (HCoV-HKU1)*	2004	Originated from Hong Kong.
Respiratory infection	*Human coronavirus NL63 (HCoV-NL63)*	2004	Originated from Amsterdam, Netherlands.[31] Likely originated from tricolored bats.
Middle East respiratory syndrome (MERS)	*Middle East respiratory syndrome–related coronavirus (MERS-CoV)*	2012	Caused outbreaks in 2012, 2015, and 2018. Likely originated from the Middle East, particularly Jeddah.
Porcine diarrhea	*HKU15*	2014	Discovered in Hong Kong.
Coronavirus disease 2019 (COVID-19)	Severe acute respiratory syndrome coronavirus 2 (SARS-CoV-2), a strain of SARSr-CoV	2019	Cause of the COVID-19 pandemic. Originated from Wuhan, China; possibly from horseshoe bats, pangolins, or both.

-

History of Corona Virus

- First described in detail in the 1960s, the Corona virus gets its name from a distinctive corona or 'Crown' of sugary-proteins that projects from the envelope surrounding the particle. Encoding the virus's make-up is the longest genome of any RNA-based virus – a single strand of nucleic acid roughly 26,000 to 32,000 bases long.

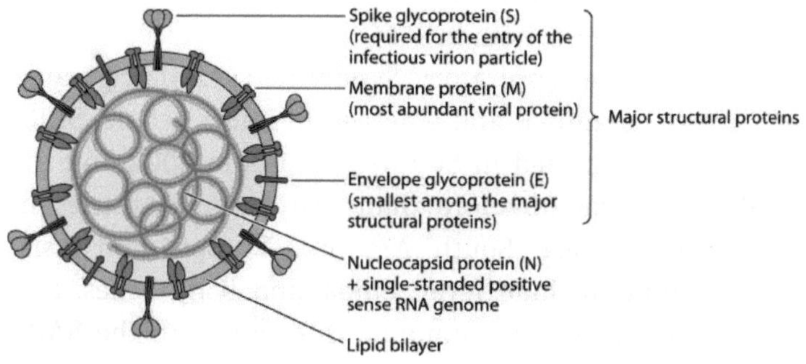

- There are different types of coronaviruses that cause respiratory and sometimes gastrointestinal symptoms.
- Respiratory disease can range from the common cold to pneumonia and in most people, the symptoms tend to be mild.
- However, there are some types of coronaviruses that can cause severe disease. These include the Severe Acute Respiratory Syndrome Coronavirus, first identified in China in 2003 and the Middle East Respiratory Syndrome Coronavirus, that was first identified in Saudi Arabia in 2012. The 2019 novel coronavirus was first identified in China.

- Middle East Respiratory Syndrome (MERS) was first reported in 2012 in Saudi Arabia and spread to more than 25 other countries. MERS originated in camels and emerged to infect people. Symptoms usually include fever, cough, and shortness of breath, and often progress to pneumonia. About 3 or 4 out of every 10 patients reported with MERS have died. MERS cases continue to occur, primarily in the Arabian Peninsula; however, as of 2019, there have been only two confirmed cases of MERS in the US, both in 2014.
- Severe Acute Respiratory Syndrome (SARS) originated in small mammal and emerged to infect people. SARS was first reported in Southern China in 2002 and the illness spread to more than two dozen countries in North America, South America, Europe, and Asia. Symptoms include fever, chills, and body aches, and may progress to pneumonia. Infection with the SARS virus causes acute respiratory distress (severe breathing difficulty), with a mortality rate of about 10 percent.
- The novel corona virus (SARS-CoV-2) that causes COVID-19 first emerged in a seafood and poultry market in the Chinese city of Wuhan in 2019.
- In December 2019, there was cluster of pneumonia cases in China. Investigations found that it was caused by a previously unknown virus – now named the 2019, novel coronavirus. It initially occurred in a group of people with pneumonia who had been associated with a seafood and live animal market, in the city of Wuhan. The disease has since spread from those who were sick to others including family members and health care staff. There are many cases at present, and the disease has spread within China and also to a number of other countries.

TWO

Corona virus Disease(COVID-19): Introduction and outbreak

Corona virus pandemic is an ongoing pandemic of coronavirus disease 2019 (COVID-19) caused by severe acute respiratory syndrome coronavirus 2 (SARS-CoV-2) which outbreak was identified in Wuhan, China, in December 2019. The World Health Organization (WHO) declared the outbreak to be a Public Health Emergency of International Concern on 30 January 2020 and recognized it as a pandemic on 11th March 2020.

It is known that coronaviruses circulate in a range of animals. Sometimes, these viruses can make the jump from animals to humans. This is called a "spillover" and could be due to a range of factors such as mutations in the virus or increased contact between humans and animals. For example, MERS CoV is known to be transmitted from camels and SARS CoV from civet cats. The animal reservoir of the 2019 novel coronavirus is not yet known.

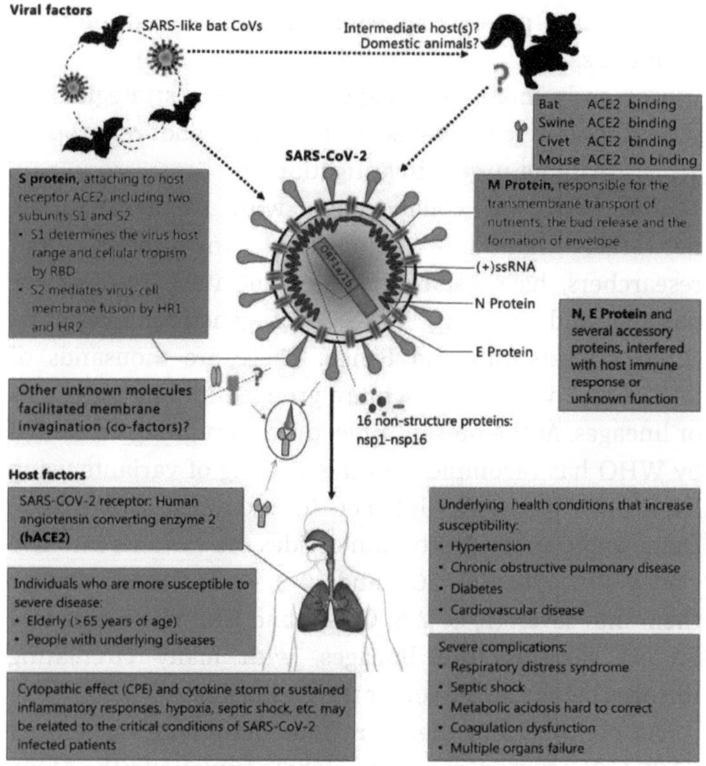

The novel coronavirus uses the same receptor, angiotensin-converting enzyme 2 (ACE2) as that for SARS-CoV, and mainly spreads through the respiratory tract. The elderly and people with underlying diseases are susceptible to infection and prone to serious outcomes, which may be associated with acute respiratory distress syndrome (ARDS) and cytokine storm.

Importantly, increasingly evidence showed sustained human-to-human transmission, along with many exported cases across the globe. The clinical symptoms of COVID-19 patients include fever, cough, fatigue and a small population of patients appeared gastrointestinal infection symptoms.

Currently, there are few specific antiviral strategies, but several potent candidates of antivirals and repurposed drugs are under urgent investigation.

The WHO, in collaboration with partners, expert networks, national authorities, institutions and researchers, have established nomenclature systems for naming and tracking SARS-CoV-2 genetic lineages by GISAID, Nextstrain and Pango. There are thousands of SARS-CoV-2 variants which are grouped into either clades or lineages. At the present time, the expert group convened by WHO has recommended the labeling of variants using letters of the Greek Alphabet, for example, Alpha, Beta, Delta, and Gamma.Nextstrain divides the variants into five clades (19A, 19B, 20A, 20B, and 20C), while GISAID divides them into seven (L, O, V, S, G, GH, and GR). The Pango tool groups variants into lineages, with many circulating lineages being classed under the B.1 lineage.

As of July 2021, there are four dominant variants of SARS-CoV-2 spreading among global populations: the Alpha Variant (formerly called the UK Variant and officially referred to as B.1.1.7), first found in London and Kent, the Beta Variant (formerly called the South Africa Variant and officially referred to as B.1.351), the Gamma Variant (formerly called the Brazil Variant and officially referred to as P.1), and the Delta Variant (formerly called the India Variant and officially referred to as B.1.617.2).

Using whole genome sequencing, epidemiology and modelling suggest the Alpha variant VUI-202012/01 (the first variant under investigation in December 2020) in the

B.1.1.7 lineage transmits more easily than some other strains.

CORONA VIRUS DISEASE (COVID-19) outbreak:

In early December 2019, an outbreak of coronavirus disease 2019 (COVID-19), caused by a novel severe acute respiratory syndrome coronavirus 2 (SARS-CoV-2), occurred in Wuhan City, Hubei Province, China.

On December 31, 2019, the China Health Authority alerted the World Health Organization (WHO) to several cases of pneumonia of unknown aetiology in Wuhan City in Hubei Province in central China. The cases had been reported since December 8, 2019, and many patients worked at or lived around the local Huanan Seafood Wholesale Market although other early cases had no exposure to this market. On January 7, a novel coronavirus, originally abbreviated as 2019-nCoV by WHO, was identified from the throat swab sample of a patient. This pathogen was later renamed as severe acute respiratory syndrome coronavirus 2 (SARS-CoV-2) by the Coronavirus Study Group and the disease was named coronavirus disease 2019 (COVID-19) by the WHO. As of 30th January 2021, 30 7736 confirmed and 12,167 suspected cases had been reported in China and 82 confirmed cases had been detected in 18 other countries. In the same day, WHO declared the SARS-CoV-2 outbreak as a Public Health Emergency of International Concern (PHEIC).

Know the facts:

- In recent decades, several new diseases have emerged in different geographical areas, with pathogens including Ebola virus, Zika virus, Nipah virus, and coronaviruses (CoVs). Recently, a new type of viral infection emerged in Wuhan City, China, and initial genomic sequencing data of this virus do not match with previously sequenced CoVs, suggesting a novel CoV strain (2019-nCoV), which has now been termed severe acute respiratory syndrome CoV-2 (SARS-CoV-2).

- Although coronavirus disease 2019 (COVID-19) is suspected to originate from an animal host (zoonotic origin) followed by human-to-human transmission, the possibility of other routes should not be ruled out.
- Compared to diseases caused by previously known human CoVs, COVID-19 shows less severe pathogenesis but higher transmission competence, as is evident from the continuously increasing number of confirmed cases globally.
- Compared to other emerging viruses, such as Ebola virus, avian H7N9, SARS-CoV, and Middle East respiratory syndrome coronavirus (MERS-CoV), SARS-CoV-2 has shown relatively low pathogenicity and moderate transmissibility.
- Codon usage studies suggest that this novel virus has been transferred from an animal source, such as bats.
- Early diagnosis by real-time PCR and next-generation sequencing has facilitated the identification of the pathogen at an early stage.
- Since no antiviral drug exists to treat or prevent SARS-CoV-2, potential therapeutic strategies that are currently being evaluated predominantly stem from previous experience with treating SARS-CoV, MERS-CoV, and other emerging viral diseases. However, some vaccines had been developed and found effective against this disease.

THREE

COVID-19: Clinical Presentation and Management

COVID-19 is a respiratory disease caused by a novel corona virus named as severe acute respiratory syndrome corona virus 2 (SARS-CoV-2) which was previously provisionally known as 2019 novel corona virus (2019-nCoV)], a new coronavirus discovered in 2019. Corona Virus Disease 2019 (COVID-19) originated in the city of Wuhan, Hubei Province, Central China, and has spread quickly to more than 72 countries to date. Corona Virus Disease 2019 (COVID-19) is suspected to originate from an animal host (zoonotic origin) followed by human-to-human transmission, the possibility of other routes should not be ruled out.

Origin of SARS-CoV-2: The initial source of SARS-CoV-2 is still unknown, although the first cases were linked to the Huanan seafood market in Wuhan city. Besides seafood, it is reported on social media that some wild animals including birds, snakes, marmots and bats were sold at the Huanan seafood market. It has been reported that environmental samples obtained from the marketplace have come back positive for the novel CoV, but the specific animal has not been identified. More recently, several studies have suggested that bats may be the potential natural host of SARS-CoV-2. The whole genome-wide nucleotide sequence of SARS-CoV-2 is 96% identical to a bat CoV. Importantly, SARS-CoV-2 has been isolated from pangolins and it was found that the isolated pangolin CoV genomes have ~85.5–92.4% similarity to SARS-CoV-2, suggesting that pangolin may be a potential intermediate host for SARS-CoV-2.

Mode of Transmission: Sometimes the COVID-19 virus can spread when a person is exposed to very small droplets or aerosols that stay in the air for several minutes or hours. This is called airborne transmission. The COVID-19 virus can spread from someone who is infected but has no symptoms. This is called asymptomatic transmission. The COVID-19 virus can also spread from someone who is infected but hasn't developed symptoms yet. This is called pre-symptomatic transmission.

Transmission route of SARS-CoV-2: COVID-19 is caused by infection with the severe acute respiratory syndrome coronavirus 2 (SARS-CoV-2) virus strain. The disease is mainly transmitted via the respiratory route when people inhale droplets and small airborne particles (that form an aerosol) that infected people exhale as they breathe, talk, cough, sneeze, or sing. Current evidence suggests that

COVID-19 spreads between people through direct, indirect (through contaminated objects or surfaces), or close contact with infected people via mouth and nose secretions. These include saliva, respiratory secretions or secretion droplets. These are released from the mouth or nose when an infected person coughs, sneezes, speaks or sings, for example. People who are in close contact (within 1 metre) with an infected person can catch COVID-19 when those infectious droplets get into their mouth, nose or eyes.

The virus can also spread if you touch a surface with the virus on it and then touch your mouth, nose or eyes. But the risk is low.

Causes of COVID-19: Infection with severe acute respiratory syndrome coronavirus 2, or SARS-CoV-2, causes coronavirus disease 2019 (COVID-19).The virus that causes COVID-19 spreads easily among people. Data has shown that the COVID-19 virus spreads mainly from person to person among those in close contact (within about 6 feet, or 2 meters) through the released virus spreads by respiratory droplets.

Signs and symptoms of COVID-19: It may appear 2 to 14 days after exposure. This time after exposure and before having symptoms is called the incubation period. You can still spread COVID-19 before you have symptoms (pre-symptomatic transmission).

Common signs and symptoms can include: Fever, Cough and Tiredness. Early symptoms of COVID-19 may include a loss of taste or smell. Other symptoms can include: Shortness of breath or difficulty breathing, Muscle aches, Chills, Sore throat, Runny nose, Headache, Chest pain, Pink eye (conjunctivitis), Nausea, Vomiting, Diarrhoea, Rash etc.

Emergency signs and symptoms can include: Trouble breathing, Persistent chest pain or pressure, Inability to stay awake, New confusion as well as Pale, gray or blue-colored skin, lips or nail beds — depending on skin tone.

An older adult or have chronic medical conditions, such as heart disease or lung disease, as you may have a greater risk of becoming seriously ill with COVID-19.

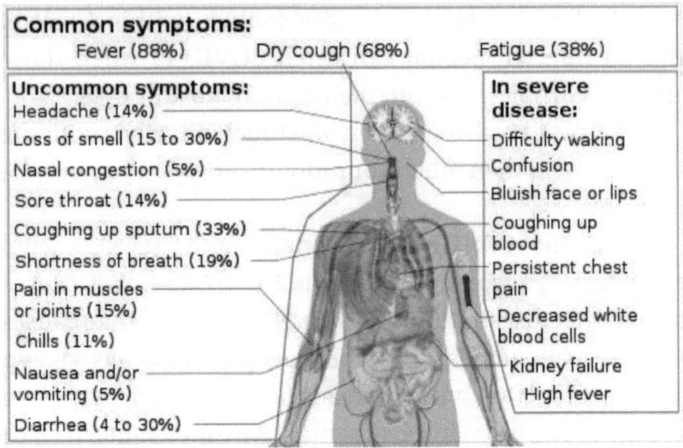

The severity of COVID-19 symptoms can range from very mild to severe. Some people may have only a few symptoms. Some people may have no symptoms at all, but can still spread it (asymptomatic transmission). Some people may experience worsened symptoms, such as worsened shortness of breath and pneumonia, about a week after symptoms start.

Some people experience COVID-19 symptoms for more than four weeks after they're diagnosed. These health issues are sometimes called post-COVID-19 conditions. Children have similar symptoms to adults and generally have mild illness. Some children experience multisystem inflammatory syndrome, a syndrome that can affect some organs and tissues, several weeks after having COVID-19. Rarely, some adults experience the syndrome too.

Risk age group: People who are older have a higher risk of serious illness from COVID-19, and the risk increases with age. People who have existing medical conditions also may have a higher risk of serious illness. Certain medical conditions that may increase the risk of serious illness from COVID-19 include:

- Serious heart diseases, such as heart failure, coronary artery disease or cardiomyopathy
- Cancer
- Chronic obstructive pulmonary disease (COPD)
- Type 1 or type 2 diabetes
- Overweight, obesity or severe obesity
- High blood pressure
- Smoking
- Chronic kidney disease
- Sickle cell disease or thalassemia
- Weakened immune system from solid organ transplants or bone marrow transplants
- Pregnancy
- Asthma
- Chronic lung diseases such as cystic fibrosis or pulmonary hypertension
- Liver disease
- Dementia
- Down syndrome
- Weakened immune system from bone marrow transplant, HIV or some medications
- Brain and nervous system conditions, such as strokes
- Substance use disorders

Risk factors: Risk factors for COVID-19 appear to include: Close contact (within 6 feet, or 2 meters) with someone who has COVID-19 or Being coughed or sneezed on by an infected person

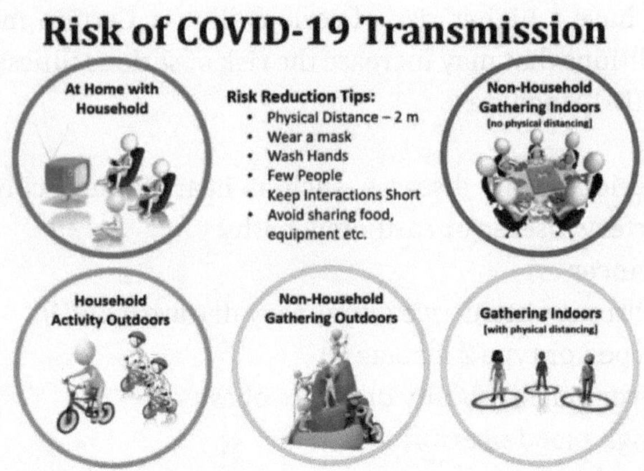

Investigation and Diagnosis: To test for the COVID-19 virus, a health care provider takes a sample from the nose (nasopharyngeal swab), throat (throat swab) or saliva. The samples are then tested at lab. If someone is coughing up sputum, then sputum can also be tested.

COVID-19 diagnostic testing is done to find out if you're currently infected with SARS-CoV-2, the virus that causes coronavirus disease 2019 (COVID-19).

The approved tests for diagnosing a COVID-19 infection are:

- **PCR test:**Also called a molecular test, this COVID-19 test detects genetic material of the virus using a lab technique called polymerase chain reaction (PCR). A fluid sample is collected by inserting a long nasal swab (nasopharyngeal swab) into your nostril and taking fluid from the back of your nose or by using a shorter nasal swab (mid-turbinate swab) to get a sample.

In some cases, a long swab is inserted into the back of your throat (oropharyngeal swab), or you may spit into a tube to produce a saliva sample. Results may be available in minutes if analyzed onsite or a few days — or longer in locations with test processing delays — if sent to an outside lab. PCR tests are very accurate when properly performed by a health care professional, but the rapid test can miss some cases.

- **Antigen test.**This COVID-19 test detects certain proteins in the virus. Using a long nasal swab to get a fluid sample, some antigen tests can produce results in minutes. Others may be sent to a lab for analysis.

A positive antigen test result is considered accurate when instructions are carefully followed, but there's an increased chance of false-negative results — meaning it's possible to be infected with the virus but have a negative result. Depending on the situation, the doctor may recommend a PCR test to confirm a negative antigen test result.

A PCR test called the Flu SC2 Multiplex Assay can detect any of three viruses at the same time: the COVID-19 virus, influenza A and influenza B (flu). Only a single sample is needed to check for all three viruses, and this could be helpful during the flu season. But a negative result does not rule out the possibility of any of these infections. So the diagnostic process may include more steps, depending on symptoms, possible exposures and your doctor's clinical judgment.

Chest CT scans may be helpful to diagnose COVID-19 in individuals with a high clinical suspicion of infection but are not recommended for routine screening.

Treatment of COVID-19: There is no specific, effective treatment or cure for Corona virus disease 2019 (COVID-19), the disease caused by the SAR-CoV-2 virus. the cornerstone of management of COVID-19 has been supportive care, which includes treatment to relieve symptoms, fluids therapy, oxygen support and prone as needed, and medications or devices to support other affected vital organs are at first line of treatment.

Complications: Although most people with COVID-19 have mild to moderate symptoms, thedisease can cause severe medical complications and lead to death in some people. Older adults or people with existing chronic medical conditions are at greater risk of becoming seriously ill with COVID-19.

Complications can include:

- Pneumonia in both lungs and
- Organ failure in several organs

Preventive Measures: In order to prevent COVID-19, self-protection and prevention is needed. Wearing mask at public places, self-isolation or quarantine, making handwash a regular habit, taking full dose of vaccination, social distancing and keeping distance of 6 feet away with other while taking etc.

FOUR

APPROVED COVID-19 VACCINES

On one hand, the world inches closer to 100% vaccination each passing day, while on the other, questions about the safety and efficacy of COVID vaccines are being raised. In such a climate, approvals from international health regulatory bodies like the WHO have become pivotal.

There are 8 vaccines that are approved for use by the WHO. Let's take a closer look at which vaccines have been approved by the World Health Organization so far.

- Pfizer/BioNTech
- Moderna
- Janssen (Johnson & Johnson)
- AstraZeneca
- Covishield
- Bharat Biotech – Covaxin
- Sinopharm (Bejing)
- Sinovac

List of COVID vaccines approved by WHO

Pfizer/BioNTech: Comirnaty

The BNT162b2 is a messenger Ribonucleic Acid (mRNA) vaccine meaning that it carries genetic instructions that help the recipient's cells to produce protein pieces that trigger immune system response.

On 31 December 2020, Comirnaty became the first vaccine to get a nod from the WHO. It has been approved in almost 100 countries across the globe, including the USA, the UK, the UAE, Saudi Arabia, Canada and Australia.

Oxford/AstraZeneca: Vaxzevria and Covishield

The ChAdOx1 COVID-19 vaccine is based on the virus's genetic instructions for building the spike protein, which is stored using double-stranded DNA.

WHO approved three versions of the AstraZeneca vaccine so far: one in the EU, one produced by Serum Institute of India (SII) and the third by SKBio (Republic of Korea) on 15 February 2021 for emergency use as well as COVAX supply. AstraZeneca is the highest distributed vaccine in the world, with 122 countries having recognized it. Covishield has been authorized by around 46 countries, including India, Egypt, Maldives, and others primarily in Asia and Africa.

Johnson & Johnson: Ad26.COV2.S

The Janssen vaccine leverages the AdVac vaccine platform to engineer a common cold virus to carry genetic instructions into the arm cells where they construct a replica of the coronavirus spike, triggering the immune system.

The one-off vaccine was listed by the WHO for emergency use and COVAX roll-out on 12 March 2021.

Around 70 countries, including Bahrain, South Africa, the USA and Kuwait have included the Janssen jabs in their immunization programs.

Moderna: Spikevax

The Moderna vaccine primarily works by injecting a fraction of the COVID-19 virus' genetic code into the body. This will trigger the body's immune response, therefore, creating antibodies capable of fighting the virus.

The WHO authorized Moderna for emergency use on 30 April 2021. The American vaccine has received approval in 76 countries, including the USA, France, Germany, Israel, Qatar, and Singapore.

Sinopharm: BBIBP-CorV

Sinopharm relies on the older but tested technology, which involves taking an inactivated form of the virus to stimulate the body's immune response.

The Chinese pharmaceutical got the green signal from the WHO on 7 May 2021. So far, 65 countries, including Argentina, China, Lebanon, Pakistan, and Vietnam.

Sinovac: CoronaVac

Sinovac, too, is an inactivated virus vaccine, which means it is made from viral particles produced in a lab, which are then inactivated so they can't infect with COVID-19.

It was approved by the WHO on 1 June 2021 and is currently being used and approved in around 40 countries including Brazil, Indonesia, the Philippines and Thailand.

Bharat Biotech: Covaxin

Covaxin is an inactivated virus-based COVID-19 vaccine developed by Bharat Biotech in collaboration with the Indian Council of Medical Research – National Institute of Virology.

In all age groups 18 and up, the WHO's Strategic Advisory Group of Experts on Immunization (SAGE) recommends using the vaccine in two doses with a four-week gap between them. Covaxin was found to have a 78 percent effectiveness against COVID-19 of any severity 14 days or more after the second dosage, and is ideal for low- and middle-income nations because to its simple storage needs.

The WHO's Strategic Advisory Group of Experts on Immunization (SAGE) has approved Covaxin for emergency use early November 2021. The vaccine is currently accepted in several countries including Mexico, Nepal, Philippines and India.

COVID-19 vaccines are now widely available for people ages 5 years and older. All currently approved or authorized COVID-19 vaccines are safe, effective and reduce risk of severe illness.

vaccine	Pfizer-BioNTech	Moderna	Johnson & Johnson's Janssen
Ages Recommended	5+ years old	18+ years old	18+ years old
Primary Series	2 doses Given 3 weeks (21 days) apart	2 doses Given 4 weeks (28 days) apart	1 dose
Booster Dose	At least 6 months after last dose in series in some people ages 18 years and older who are at higher risk for COVID-19 exposure or severe illness. Any of the three COVID-19 vaccines can be used for the booster dose.	At least 6 months after last dose in series in some people ages 18 years and older who are at higher risk for COVID-19 exposure or severe illness. Any of the three COVID-19 vaccines can be used for the booster dose.	At least 2 months after first dose in all people ages 18 years and older. Any of the three COVID-19 vaccines can be used for the booster dose.
When Fully Vaccinated	2 weeks after 2nd dose	2 weeks after 2nd dose	2 weeks after 1st dose
Note: If you had a severe allergic reaction (anaphylaxis) after a previous dose or if you have a known (diagnosed) allergy to a COVID-19 vaccine ingredient, you should not get that vaccine. If you have been instructed not to get one type of COVID-19 vaccine, you may still be able to get another type.			

Additional recommendations for Immunocompromised people:

Additional primary dose: Moderately to severely immunocompromised people who are 12 years and older and received a Pfizer-BioNTech primary series or 18 years and older and received a Moderna primary series should receive an additional primary dose of the same vaccine at least 28 days after their second dose.

Booster dose: Moderately to severely immunocompromised people who are 18 years of age and older and received a Pfizer-BioNTech or Moderna primary series are also eligible for a booster dose at least 6 months after their additional primary dose, using any of the three COVID-19 vaccines.

Immunocompromised people who received a J&J/ Janssen vaccine are not recommended to receive an additional primary dose, but should receive a booster dose at least 2 months after their initial dose, using any of the three COVID-19 vaccines.

FIVE

COVID-19 AND BASIC PREVENTIVE METHOD

This new virus (COVID-19 virus) currently has a limited geographic spread.However, there are a number of standard hygiene practises that have been recommended to protect against infection and further spread. These include: Covering your mouth and nose when coughing or sneezing with a medical mask, tissue or
flexed elbow; Avoiding close contact with those who are unwell; the appropriate use of masks and Personal ProtectiveEquipment (PPE) – especially in a health care setting; Washing hands regularly with soap and water or alcohol-based hand rub.
Actions that can be taken to prevent infection from an animal source include: Avoiding unnecessary unprotected contact with animals; washing hands after contact with

animals or animal products and; ensuring that animals products are cooked thoroughly before they are consumed.

Although no specific medicine and treatment is available for COVID-19 but we can take steps to reduce your risk of infection. WHO and CDC recommend following these precautions for avoiding COVID-19:

- Avoid large events and mass gatherings.
- Avoid close contact (within about 6 feet, or 2 meters) with anyone who is sick or has symptoms.
- Keep distance between yourself and others if COVID-19 is spreading in your community, especially if you have a higher risk of serious illness.
- Wash your hands often with soap and water for at least 20 seconds, or use an alcohol- based hand sanitizer that contains at least 60% alcohol.
- Cover your mouth and nose with your elbow or a tissue when you cough or sneeze. Throw used tissues in the trash and then wash your hands with soap and water for at least 20 seconds.
- Avoid touching your eyes, nose and mouth.
- Avoid sharing dishes, glasses, bedding and other household items if you're sick.
- Clean and disinfect high-touch surfaces daily.
- Stay home from work, school and public areas if you're sick, unless you're going to get medical care. Avoid taking public transportation if you're sick.

SOME OTHER PREVENTION TIPS:

- Get a COVID-19 vaccine if you are 12 or older. COVID-19 vaccines are safe, effective, and free!

- Avoid close contact with people outside your home. Stay at least 6 feet (about 2 arms' length) from others.
- Wear a mask in public, even if you don't feel sick. The make cover will help protect others in case you are infected.
- Clean and disinfect frequently touched surfaces daily. This includes tables, doorknobs, light switches, countertops, handles, desks, phones, keyboards, toilets, faucets, and sinks.
- Stay home if you have symptoms such as fever, cough, shortness of breath.
- Seek emergency medical care if you develop severe symptoms, such as trouble breathing, chest pain, new confusion, inability to wake or stay awake, or pale, gray, or blue-colored skin, lips, or nail beds, depending on skin tone.

How to Handwash?

WASH HANDS WHEN VISIBLY SOILED! OTHERWISE, USE HANDRUB

Duration of the entire procedure: 40-60 seconds

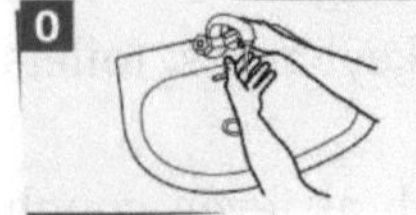

Wet hands with water;

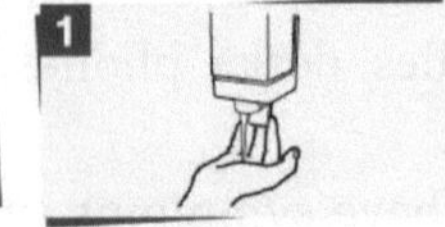

Apply enough soap to cover all hand surfaces;

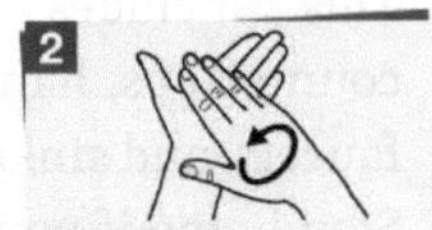

Rub hands palm to palm;

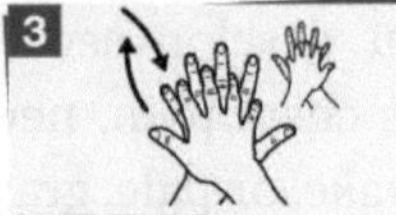

Right palm over left dorsum with interlaced fingers and vice versa;

Palm to palm with fingers interlaced;

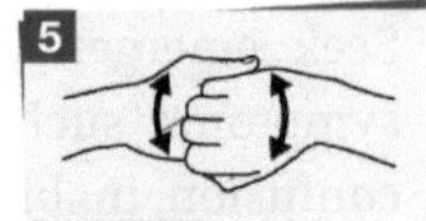

Backs of fingers to opposing palms with fingers interlocked;

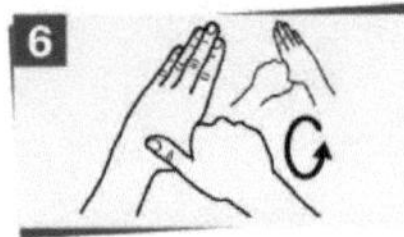

Rotational rubbing of left thumb clasped in right palm and vice versa;

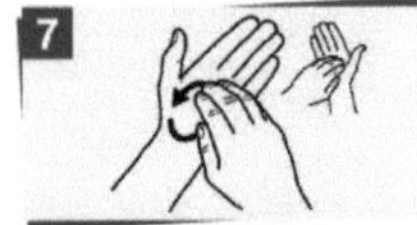

Rotational rubbing, backwards and forwards with clasped fingers of right hand in left palm and vice versa;

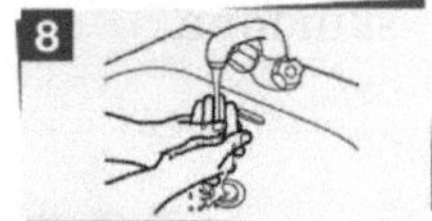

Rinse hands with water;

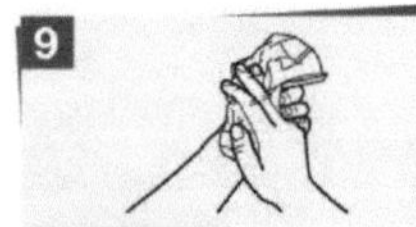

Dry hands thoroughly with a single use towel;

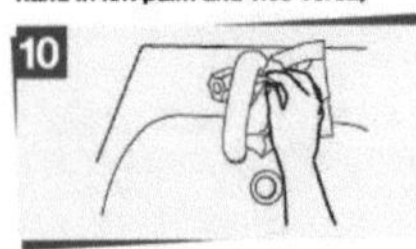

Use towel to turn off faucet;

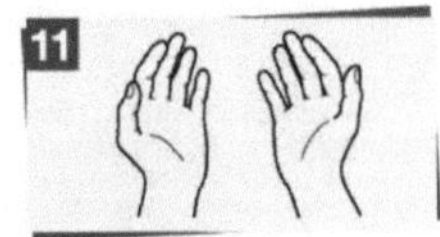

Your hands are now safe.

Patient Safety

A World Alliance for Safer Health Care

SAVE LIVES

Clean Your Hands

How to Handrub?

RUB HANDS FOR HAND HYGIENE! WASH HANDS WHEN VISIBLY SOILED

Duration of the entire procedure: 20-30 seconds

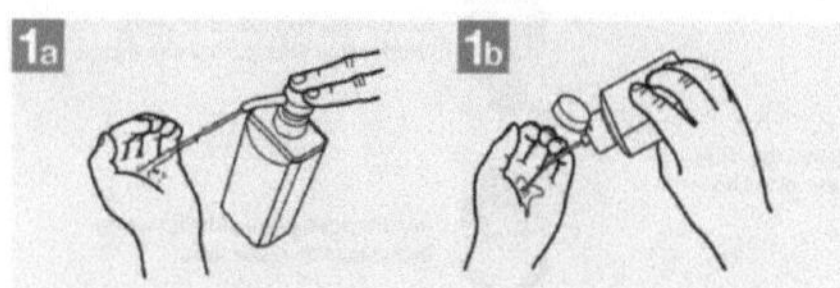

Apply a palmful of the product in a cupped hand, covering all surfaces;

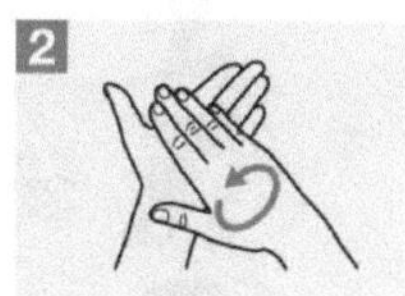

Rub hands palm to palm;

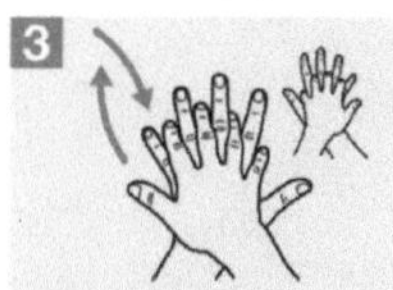

Right palm over left dorsum with interlaced fingers and vice versa;

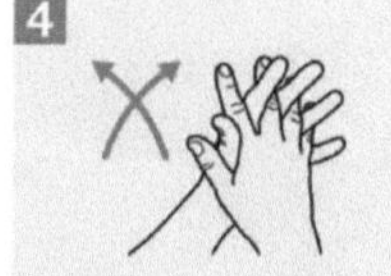

Palm to palm with fingers interlaced;

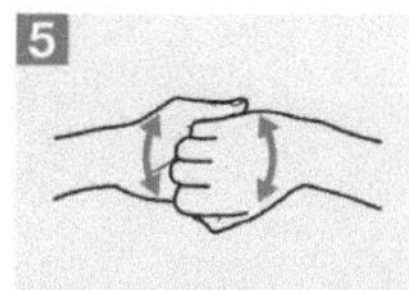

Backs of fingers to opposing palms with fingers interlocked;

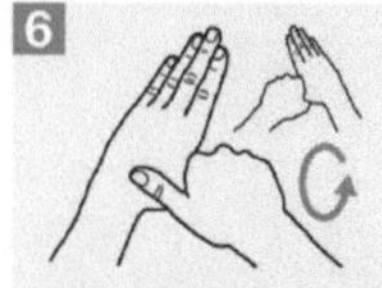

Rotational rubbing of left thumb clasped in right palm and vice versa;

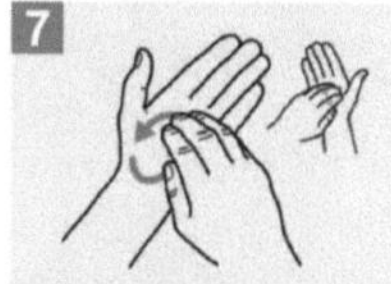

Rotational rubbing, backwards and forwards with clasped fingers of right hand in left palm and vice versa;

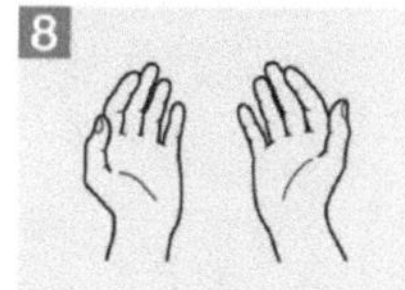

Once dry, your hands are safe.

World Health Organization

Patient Safety

A World Alliance for Safer Health Care

SAVE LIVES

Clean **Your** Hands

DO choose masks that

- Have two or more layers of washable, breathable fabric
- Completely cover your nose and mouth
- Fit snugly against the sides of your face and don't have gaps
- Have a nose wire to prevent air from leaking out of the top of the mask

DO NOT choose masks that

- Are made of fabric that makes it hard to breathe, for example, vinyl
- Have exhalation valves or vents, which allow virus particles to escape
- Are intended for healthcare workers, including N95 respirators

CDC

cdc.gov/coronavirus

SIX

Healthcare Professional and Covid-19

SEVEN

COVID-19 AND MENSURATION

COVID-19 AND MENSTRUATION

Scientists don't know the answer regarding covid-19 affecting period but they're starting to study the issue. Vaccines are designed to activate immune system, and some experts have wondered if that could temporarily disrupt menstrual cycles. So far, reports of irregular bleeding after getting a COVID-19 vaccine have been anecdotal and it's hard to draw any direct links to the vaccines since changes could be the result of other factors including stress, diet and exercise habits.

A few days after the Government of India announced scaling up inoculation against the Covid-19 infection by allowing all above 18 years of age to take their vaccines from May 1, several women have raised concerns over taking Covid-19 vaccination during periods [menstruation]. The concerns were triggered after a claim, widely circulating on social media platforms, said that women should not take Covid-19 vaccines five days before and after their period cycle. The social media post claimed that women should not take vaccines five days before or after their periods as their "immunity is very less" during periods. As fake posts on vaccine unsafe during menstruation started spreading, the Government of India has come forward to educate that this claim is fake. Vaccination for all above the ages of 18 can be done from May 1st, 2021. The clarification came as fake messages started taking rounds on social media websites. The government, through Press Information Bureau (PIB) fact check, appealed to citizens to not fall on such unfounded rumor-mongering. Several doctors also came out to throw that there is no culpable evidence connecting the efficacy of vaccines or its supposed dangers during a women's menstruation cycle. Doctors and activists, too, have quashed the claims, saying periods have nothing to do with the vaccinations.

Most of the Gynecologist believed that The benefits of taking the vaccine certainly way outweigh putting up with one heavy period, if indeed they're related. In a New York Times article, Alice Lu-Culligan and Randi Hutter Epstein at Yale School of Medicine also debunked the claim and said that So far, there's no data linking the vaccines to changes in menstruation."Even if there is a connection, one unusual period is no cause for alarm," they said.

Missed periods during the course of infection, irregular cycles after recovery, spotting, heavy flows, abnormally longer period duration are some of the issues women have reported related to their menstrual cycle amid pandemic. Delayed periods or irregular flow are often associated with stress and anxiety. "Stress is directly associated with women's menstrual patterns. It has so much to do with female hormones, uneven cycle, pain during periods, mood swings, unnecessary fatigue etc. Hence it's not surprising if women are complaining about such experiences. Also, women are forced to manage household work and office work together, many even don't get a helping hand at home. Hence, stress generated in such environments can massively affect a woman's overall wellbeing including menstrual patterns.

One of reputated Gynecologist and IVF specialist said "Stress itself is well-known to cause period irregularities by disrupting the hypothalamic-pituitary ovarian axis- the hormonal system the brain uses to speak to the ovaries. Stress also causes hormonal imbalance and even PCOS (Polycystic Ovary Syndrome) in women. If you had been borderline PCOS all along, this stress induced by the pandemic might push you over to the other side."

It is also believed that it could be a stress-induced temporary change, "blood clots bleeding/heavy bleeding was found in people post-Covid". "Since Covid affects many organs of the body including intestines, kidneys, walls of the artery which affects one's blood pressure, in women, what happens is when you have inflammation in the body, the blood vessels swell up which does not let the blood release. We don't have a lot of research around menstrual cycles in general. And till now, Covid and the menstrual cycle have not been studied, so, therefore, there is no clarity yet,"

"As whole body is coping with the pressure of Covid infection and in recovering stage, one can very well expect that it will interfere in your cycles, too. Stress can increase the imbalance of insulin in the body which causes the secretion of the leptin hormone. Women who used to cycle period within the first 30 days, now their cycle can be delayed by 7-8 days or even more. This is called oligomenorrhea," said senior consultant, gynecologist and IVF specialist from top hospital of Delhi NCR.

Knowing the fact that Healthy lifestyle, which includes regular exercises and balanced diet is the most important factor in women's health. Weight-bearing exercises keep bones strong and weight in check which prevents hormonal imbalances," she said. Obesity leads to an increase in lipid profile which affects the menstrual hormone ratio. Even in PCOD, increased fat increases the level of testosterone hormone which surely affects the right ratio of female hormones.

Experts recommend one key factor in reducing stress levels is coming to terms with the fact that the current situation is not in anyone's hands, and working on oneself is really the best way to deal with it. Try and make a fixed routine for your day, eat healthy foods, sleep on time, and try to be happy as much as possible. Do not take stress unnecessarily. Help is there and do not panic.

Some tips to cope with these conditions related to periods in female in this pandemic can be well described as:

*__Positive outlook__— Although the situation is tough, we all are supposed to fight back. It is alright to get mentally affected by the pandemic but it is also necessary to maintain mental sanity. Keep your mental health prime which is associated with one's overall wellbeing.

*__Meditation__— Make a schedule for meditation. Take some peaceful time out of your schedule to calm your mind down. It helps to rejuvenate the mind. Pranayama, breathing exercises can help.

*__Nutrition__— Take good care of nutrition. Avoid eating unhealthy. Lack of nutrition can make you anaemic which can affect bleeding patterns during periods. Take iron and calcium-rich food.

*__Exercise__— As a sedentary lifestyle has already somehow restricted body movement, one should balance it with exercises. There are exercises which can be done in confined rooms. Do stationary jogging in front of an open window; opt for some yoga postures under the proper supervision of an expert.

*__E-consultation__— Many of us are fortunate to have an internet connection and necessary gadgets at home. Hence, make the best use of it for your health. Be in touch with your doctor through online platforms if already suffering from any severe disease.

It is apt to let your doctor know that you have had some menstrual irregularities. They may wish to perform some tests such as blood counts to check for anaemia, possible pregnancy or thyroid disorder. Never ignore uneven menstrual cycle. If you are experiencing heavy bleeding, spotting, unnecessary fatigue, abnormal delay in period dates, then consult a doctor and start the prescribed treatment without delay.

****************** Ritesh Mishra *********************

World Health Organization : Posters

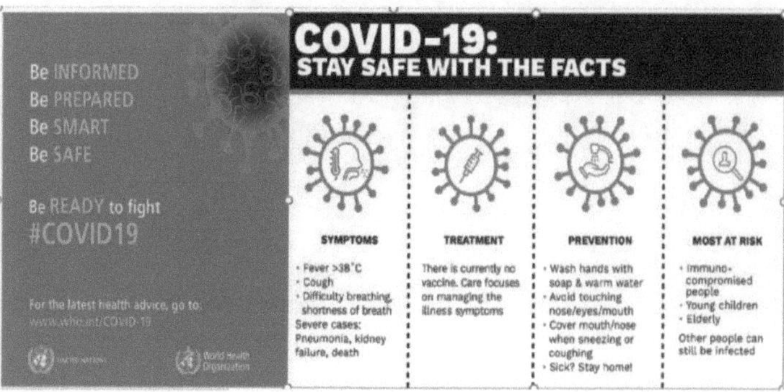

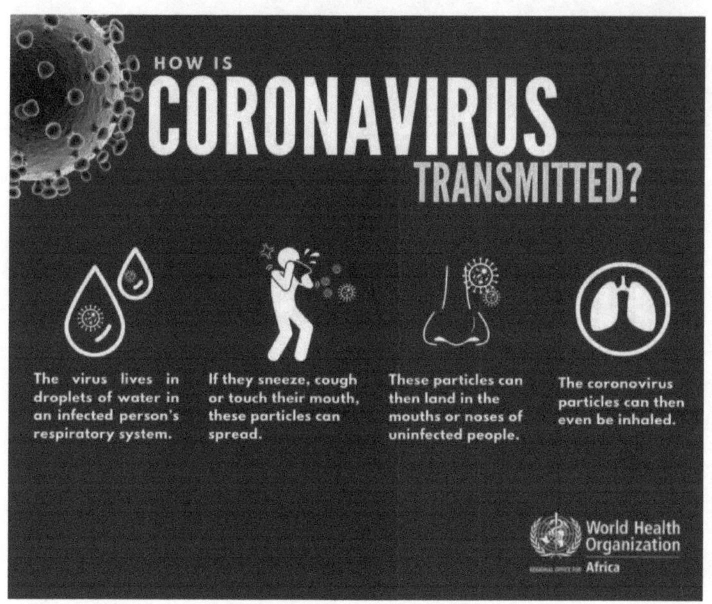

How effective are thermal scanners in detecting people infected with the new coronavirus?

Thermal scanners are effective in detecting people who have developed a fever (i.e. have a higher than normal body temperature) because of infection with the new coronavirus.

However, they cannot detect people who are infected but are not yet sick with fever. This is because it takes between 2 and 10 days before people who are infected become sick and develop a fever.

World Health Organization

#2019nCoV

Are antibiotics effective in preventing and treating the new coronavirus?

No, antibiotics do not work against viruses, only bacteria.

The new coronavirus (2019-nCOV) is a virus and, therefore, antibiotics should not be used as a means of prevention or treatment.

However, if you are hospitalized for the 2019-nCoV, you may receive antibiotics since bacterial co-infection is possible.

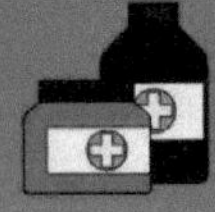

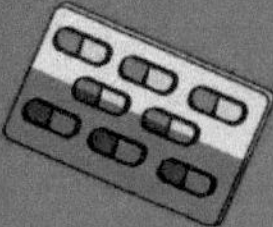

World Health Organization

#Coronavirus

No. Hand dryers are not effective in killing the 2019-nCoV.
To protect yourself against the new coronavirus, you should frequently clean your hands with an alcohol-based hand rub or wash them with soap and water. Once your hands are cleaned, you should dry them thoroughly by using paper towels or a warm air dryer.

#2019nCoV

Are hand dryers effective in killing the new coronavirus?

Is wearing rubber gloves while out in public effective in preventing the new coronavirus infection?

No. Regularly washing your bare hands offers more protection against catching COVID-19 than wearing rubber gloves.
You can still pick up COVID-19 contamination on rubber gloves.
If you then touch your face, the contamination goes from your glove to your face and can infect you.

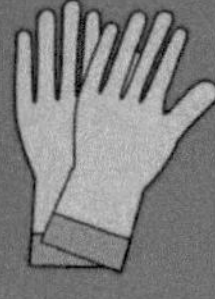

#Coronavirus #COVID19

Does the new coronavirus affect older people, or are younger people also susceptible?

People of all ages can be infected by the new coronavirus (nCoV-2019). **Older people, and people with pre-existing medical conditions (such as asthma, diabetes, heart disease) appear to be more vulnerable to becoming severely ill with the virus. WHO advise people of all ages to take steps to protect themselves from the virus, for example by following good hygiene and good respiratory hygiene.**

#Coronavirus

Do vaccines against pneumonia protect you against the new coronavirus?

No. Vaccines against pneumonia, such as pneumococcal vaccine and Haemophilus influenza type B (Hib) vaccine, do not provide protection against the new coronavirus.

The virus is so new and different that it needs its own vaccine. Researchers are trying to develop a vaccine against 2019-nCoV, and WHO is supporting their efforts.

Although these vaccines are not effective against 2019-nCoV, vaccination against respiratory illnesses is highly recommended to protect your health.

#2019nCoV

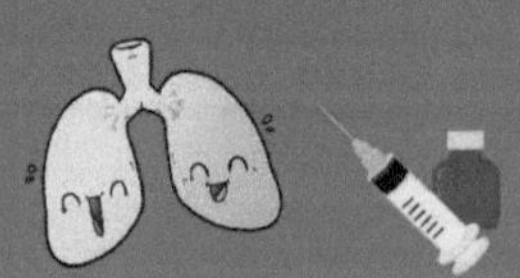

Are there any specific medicines to prevent or treat COVID-19?

To date, there is no specific medicine recommended to prevent or treat COVID-19.
However, those infected with the virus should receive appropriate care to relieve and treat symptoms, and those with severe illness should receive optimized supportive care.
Some specific treatments are under investigation, and will be tested through clinical trials
WHO is helping to accelerate research and development efforts with a range of partners.

PAHO #COVID19

Does the new coronavirus affect older people, or are younger people also susceptible?

People of all ages can be infected by the new coronavirus (nCoV-2019).
Older people, and people with pre-existing medical conditions (such as asthma, diabetes, heart disease) appear to be more vulnerable to becoming severely ill with the virus.
WHO advise people of all age to take steps to protect themselves from the virus, for example by following good hand hygiene and good respiratory hygiene.

World Health Organization #Coronavirus

Do pregnant women with suspected or confirmed COVID-19 need to give birth by caesarean section ?

- No. WHO advice is that caesarean sections should only be performed when medically justified.The mode of birth should be individualized and based on a woman's preferences along-side obstetric indications

NATHEALTH®
Healthcare Federation of India

SRC : World Health Organization

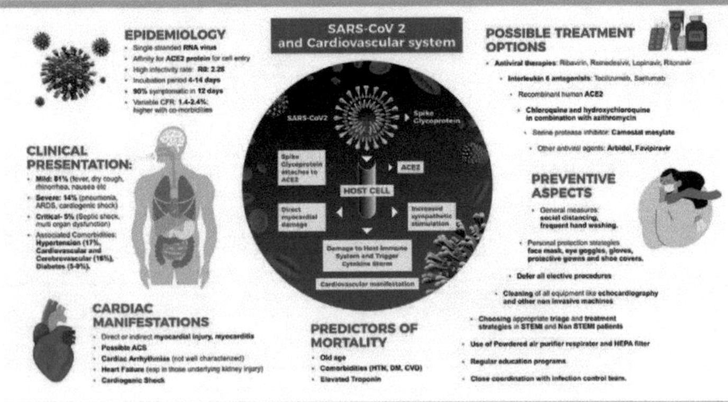

Centers For Disease Control And Prevention: Poster

How to Wear and Take Off a Non-Medical Mask or Cloth Face Covering

To Put It On

1. Wash your hands for 20 seconds with soap and water or use an alcohol-based hand rub

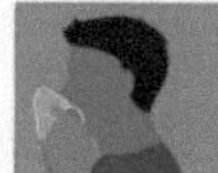

2. Put mask over your nose and mouth and secure it under your chin (do not touch the inside of the mask that will be against your face)

3. Try to fit it securely against your face

4. Tie the strings behind your head or stretch the elastic loops over your ears

5. Make sure you can breathe easily

To Take It Off

1. Untie the strings behind your head or stretch the loops over your ears

2. Handle only the ties or the loops of the mask

3. Fold the ouside corners making sure not to touch the outside of the mask

4. Place mask in a separate bag until you can get to a place where you can wash it with bleach solution

5. Wash your hands with water and soap for 20 seconds or use an alcohol-based hand rub

Using a Mask or Cloth Face Covering

1. Always keep the mask on your face and stay 2 m apart from people you do not live with

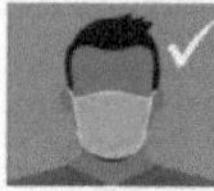

2. Ensure the mask is covering your mouth and nose

3. Do not touch the mask. If you do, wash your hands for 20 seconds

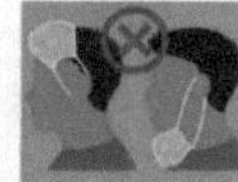

4. Do not put the mask around your neck or up on your forehead

Check with health authorities for **information and recommendations on community actions** designed to limit exposure to COVID-19.

CDC.GOV/CORONAVIRUS

How to Collect an Anterior Nasal Swab Specimen for COVID-19 Testing

Use **only** an authorized specimen collection kit given to you by your healthcare provider or personnel at the testing center, or purchased over the counter in a pharmacy or other store. Follow the instructions included with the specimen collection kit which may be used on-site or at home. Use **only** materials provided in the kit to collect and store or mail the specimen, unless the kit says to do otherwise. These instructions can also be used with self-testing kits if the kit specifies anterior nasal swab collection.

Set-up

1. Disinfect the surface where you will open the collection kit. Remove and lay out contents of kit. Read instructions before starting specimen collection.

2. Wash hands with soap and water. If soap and water are not available, use hand sanitizer.

Specimen collection

3. Remove the swab from the package. Do not touch the soft end with your hands or anything else.

4. Insert the entire soft end of the swab into your nostril **no more than ¾ of an inch** (1.5 cm) into your nose.

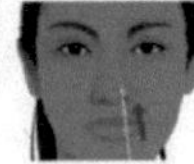

5. Slowly rotate the swab, gently pressing against the inside of your nostril at least 4 times for a total of 15 seconds. Get as much nasal discharge as possible on the soft end of the swab.

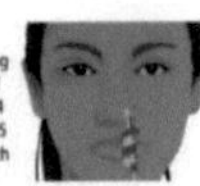

6. Gently remove the swab.

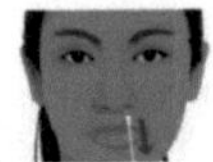

7. Using the same swab, repeat steps 4-6 in your other nostril with the same end of the swab.

Preparation of specimen for return

8. Place the swab in the sterile tube and snap off the end of the swab at the break line, so that it fits comfortably in the tube. Place the cap on the tube and screw down tightly to prevent leakage.

9. Wash hands or re-apply hand sanitizer.

10. Place the tube containing the swab in the biohazard bag provided and seal the bag.

Returning the specimen and clean-up

11. Give the bag with the swab to testing personnel or follow the instructions for returning the specimen for testing.

12. Throw away the remaining specimen collection kit items.

13. Wash hands or re-apply hand sanitizer.

What Your Test Results Mean

Accessible version available at https://www.cdc.gov/coronavirus/2019-ncov/testing/diagnostic-testing.html

If you test positive for COVID-19

TAKE STEPS TO PROTECT OTHERS REGARDLESS OF YOUR COVID-19 VACCINATION STATUS

STAY HOME.
Isolate at home for at least 10 days. Stay in a specific room and away from other people in your home.

STAY IN TOUCH WITH YOUR DOCTOR.
Contact your doctor as soon as possible if you are an older adult or have underlying medical conditions.

GET REST AND STAY HYDRATED.
If you develop symptoms, continue to isolate for at least 10 days after symptoms began and until you do not have a fever without using medications to reduce fever.

CONTACT YOUR DOCTOR OR HEALTH DEPARTMENT ABOUT ISOLATION IF YOU

- Are severely ill or have a weakened immune system.
- Had a positive test result followed by a negative result.
- Test positive for many weeks.

If you test negative for COVID-19:

- The virus was not detected.

If you have symptoms of COVID-19:

- You may have received a false negative test result and still might have COVID-19.
- Isolate from others.

If you do not have symptoms of COVID-19 and you were exposed to a person with COVID-19:

- You are likely not infected, but you still may get sick.
- Contact your doctor about your symptoms, about follow-up testing, and how long to isolate.
- Self-quarantine for 14 days at home after your exposure.
- If you are fully vaccinated, you do not need to self quarantine.
- Contact your doctor or local health department regarding options to reduce the length of your quarantine.

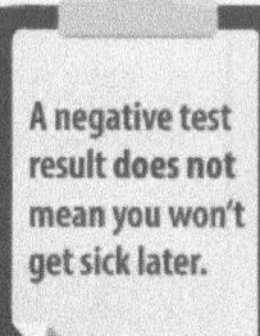

SEQUENCE FOR PUTTING ON PERSONAL PROTECTIVE EQUIPMENT (PPE)

The type of PPE used will vary based on the level of precautions required, such as standard and contact, droplet or airborne infection isolation precautions. The procedure for putting on and removing PPE should be tailored to the specific type of PPE.

1. GOWN

- Fully cover torso from neck to knees, arms to end of wrists, and wrap around the back
- Fasten in back of neck and waist

2. MASK OR RESPIRATOR

- Secure ties or elastic bands at middle of head and neck
- Fit flexible band to nose bridge
- Fit snug to face and below chin
- Fit-check respirator

3. GOGGLES OR FACE SHIELD

- Place over face and eyes and adjust to fit

4. GLOVES

- Extend to cover wrist of isolation gown

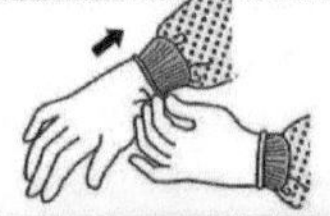

USE SAFE WORK PRACTICES TO PROTECT YOURSELF AND LIMIT THE SPREAD OF CONTAMINATION

- Keep hands away from face
- Limit surfaces touched
- Change gloves when torn or heavily contaminated
- Perform hand hygiene

SEQUENCE FOR REMOVING PERSONAL PROTECTIVE EQUIPMENT (PPE)

Except for respirator, remove PPE at doorway or in anteroom. Remove respirator after leaving patient room and closing door.

1. GLOVES

- Outside of gloves is contaminated!
- Grasp outside of glove with opposite gloved hand; peel off
- Hold removed glove in gloved hand
- Slide fingers of ungloved hand under remaining glove at wrist
- Peel glove off over first glove
- Discard gloves in waste container

2. GOGGLES OR FACE SHIELD

- Outside of goggles or face shield is contaminated!
- To remove, handle by head band or ear pieces
- Place in designated receptacle for reprocessing or in waste container

3. GOWN

- Gown front and sleeves are contaminated!
- Unfasten ties
- Pull away from neck and shoulders, touching inside of gown only
- Turn gown inside out
- Fold or roll into a bundle and discard

4. MASK OR RESPIRATOR

- Front of mask/respirator is contaminated — DO NOT TOUCH!
- Grasp bottom, then top ties or elastics and remove
- Discard in waste container

PERFORM HAND HYGIENE BETWEEN STEPS IF HANDS BECOME CONTAMINATED AND IMMEDIATELY AFTER REMOVING ALL PPE

COVID-19 Personal Protective Equipment (PPE) for Healthcare Personnel

Preferred PPE – Use N95 or Higher Respirator

Face shield or goggles

N95 or higher respirator
When respirators are not available, use the best available alternative, like a facemask.

One pair of clean, non-sterile gloves

Isolation gown

Acceptable Alternative PPE – Use Facemask

Face shield or goggles

Facemask
N95 or higher respirators are preferred but facemasks are an acceptable alternative.

One pair of clean, non-sterile gloves

Isolation gown

CDC

cdc.gov/COVID19

Message From Author

This Book is designed from the data and information collected from the reliable and authentic sources like World HealthOrganization (WHO) , Centers for Disease Control and Prevention (CDC) and various other governments sites.

The aim of this book is to aware people by providing basic information about Corona virus Disease (COVID-19) to fight against COVID-19 strongly by adopting preventive measures and promoting health. However the virus and information on the subject get updated from the responsible agencies from time to time. so, dear readers are also adviced to keep themselves updated with the information regarding ongoing pandemic.

Kindly consult your healthcare provider (physician) incase you feel any symptoms.

Stay safe and Stay healthy.

Thank you.

9 798885 037563

Printed by Libri Plureos GmbH in Hamburg,
Germany